# BEAUTIFUL
# BRITISH COLUMBIA
# WILDLIFE

| | |
|---|---|
| Creative Direction & Photo Selection: | Karl Spreitz |
| Production & Coordination: | Tony Owen |
| Text: | Anne Mayhew |
| Art Assistance: | Lyn Quan |
| Editorial Assistance: | Phil Atkinson, Rick Dykun, Bryan McGill |
| Illustration: | Edith Osborn Corbett |
| Front Cover: | Cougar beside ponderosa pine, Rocky Mountain Trench. Thomas Kitchin photograph. |
| Inside Front cover: | Grizzly bears in the Canadian Rockies. Thomas Kitchin photograph. |
| Inside Back cover: | White-tailed deer, British Columbia. Thomas Kitchin photograph. |
| Typesetting: | BCFA Publications Ltd. Ewan Edwards ($e^2$) |
| Acknowledgements: | Special thanks to Dennis Demarchi and John Youds, BC Environment |

Published by Beautiful British Columbia Magazine, a Division of Jim Pattison International Ltd. All rights reserved. No part of this edition may be reproduced in any way without written permission from the publishers.

To order copies of this book call 1-800-663-7611 in Canada or (604) 384-5456 worldwide. Fax: (604) 384-2812.
Beautiful British Columbia Magazine,
929 Ellery Streeet, Victoria, B.C., V9A 7B4.

Printed and bound in Hong Kong

**Canadian Cataloguing in Publication Data**
**Main entry under title:**
**Beautiful British Columbia wildlife**

ISBN 0-920431-05-4 (paperback)
ISBN 0-920431-06-2 (case)

1. Zoology—British Columbia. I. Beautiful British Columbia Magazine (Firm).
QL221.B7B42 1991   591.9711   C91-091458-3

# BEAUTIFUL
# BRITISH COLUMBIA
# WILDLIFE

## A Living Landscape

BEAUTIFUL
BRITISH COLUMBIA

# BEAUTIFUL
# BRITISH COLUMBIA
# WILDLIFE

## *A Living Landscape*

## INTRODUCTION

British Columbia is one of the last great wildernesses of the world. In 1873, young trailblazer Michael Phillipps made his first trip through what is now the Crowsnest Pass in the Rocky Mountains, over into the Elk River country, which was "full of game, the river full of fish." The experience was so wonderful, he likened it to a picnic, and he never left.

There are still some areas of British Columbia untouched since Phillipps' day, penetrated only here and there with ribbons of highway; and the Elk Valley itself was recently evaluated as *the* prime recreational area of North America. Northwest of the Crowsnest, cradled by the Rockies and the Columbia Mountains, lie the Columbia marshlands, a superb wildlife habitat, breeding and staging area for ducks and geese, where more than 270 species of birds have been recorded.

The whole area of the Rocky Mountain Trench is one of the prime ungulate (hoofed animal) habitats on the continent, known as the "Serengeti of the West." Here, elk, deer, black bears, coyotes, are still seen easily along the roadways. Off the road and into the wilderness a ways are moose, bighorn sheep, mountain goats, grizzlies, cougars, wolves. Make a campsite almost anywhere, and chipmunks will steal your toast, while grey jays or "whiskey jacks" will take the bacon from your pan.

From the big government ferries linking Vancouver Island and the mainland, pods of "orca," or killer whales, are still commonly seen, along with dolphins and seals, and, above water, phalaropes, pigeon guillemots, eagles, and herons. In all there are over two dozen marine mammal species off the coast. Twice a year, nearly all the world's Pacific grey whales — about 21,000 — do a sail past. More than a million birds migrate through on the Pacific flyway, and hundreds of thousands stop to nest.

More wild animal species exist in British Columbia than in any other part of Canada. A checklist of British Columbia vertebrates shows 143 mammals, 448 birds, 19 reptiles, and 20 amphibians. If the 453 species of fish were included, the total would come to 1,083 different species. Many of these species can be seen from over 60 new Wildlife Viewing Areas located throughout the province.

However, wilderness in British Columbia — at least wilderness enough to suit many species — is seldom far from the average backyard. The *Checklist of Victoria Birds* lists an astonishing 331 species in and around the capital city. And usually a cougar or two per winter finds itself loping about the residential streets of that proverbially civilized town.

About seven minutes south of Vancouver International Airport — as the heron flies — is Reifel Bird Sanctuary, on Westham Island at the mouth of the Fraser River. A good 230 species have

*Great blue heron, Capilano riverbed.*

7

THOMAS KITCHIN

*Elk, Rocky Mountains.*

This book has been conceived by Karl Spreitz, *Beautiful British Columbia Magazine's* creative director, as a "sensitive, warm embrace of our precious wildlife within their habitat and our landscape." Karl has been photographing and making films in British Columbia for 30 years, and *Wildlife* grows out of his feelings for this living landscape. He notes, "Recent improvements in photographic equipment and film stock have let us get closer and closer to the animals, but at the same time, farther away, because we have lost the sense of the animal in its own surroundings." Close-ups can give a sense of unreality, a zoolike approach to nature. It seemed time to back off a bit, reassess the value of the long shot. Accordingly, this is also a book about habitats, homes, nurturing environments.

Focusing thus on the larger view, we have let landscape be the guide in arranging these photographs. Ecologists have developed a complex system of biogeoclimatic zones named for the dominant tree species found in each zone. So there is a Coastal Western Hemlock Biogeoclimatic Zone, an Interior Douglas-fir Zone, a Ponderosa Pine/Bunchgrass Zone, and so on. In all, 12 forest zones, plus two non-forested zones, are currently recognized by the provincial Ministry of Forests.

We have taken a gentler approach, dividing the province broadly into five easy environments: the COAST, the DRYLANDS, the WETLANDS, the MOUNTAINS, the NORTH. Except for the Coast and the North, these are not geographical divisions, but descriptive divisions, particularly descriptive of climate. There are mountains throughout the province,

passed through the sanctuary, including rare birds of prey like the gyrfalcon and the Arctic rough-legged hawk that follow the flight paths of migrating geese and ducks. An astonishing 40,000 snow geese return to Reifel every autumn.

From the metropolis of Vancouver, it takes just over four hours to drive through four climatic zones — a climate an hour — to reach dry desert, near Osoyoos. From the coast, through the fertile flatlands of the Fraser River Valley; then into the mountains of Manning Park; and, dropping down into Princeton for the first whiff of sagebrush, through the oasis of Keremeos, to the little desert between Oliver and Osoyoos. Each small climate along the way shelters, nourishes, and protects its own ark of animals, birds, amphibians, and reptiles. The same rainbow of climatic zones is continued throughout the province, as mountain range becomes river valley becomes mountain range, in this "sea of mountains."

from the Rockies to the Coast range. They tend to support the same vegetation and the same wildlife. The key is the similar climate, similar elevation.

Some animals are zone specific, but some are "Everywhere Animals," like black bears and cougars, and can be found in almost any area. Grizzlies live in mountainous areas throughout the province (with the exception of Vancouver Island and the Queen Charlotte Islands): we've chosen to feature them in the north. Moose appear in both mountains and wetlands, but as they love wading into the marshes to escape summer heat, while browsing on the watery vegetation, they will be found in the wetlands.

This book will cover animals unique to British Columbia, like the mysterious white Kermode bear and the endangered Vancouver Island marmot. It will also give due attention to the "Superstars," the eagles and wolves, the killer whales, bighorn sheep, grizzlies, black bears, moose, and cougars.

It should be borne in mind that these stunning photographs are not presented to suggest naively that all is completely well in paradise. The British Columbia wilderness is in a fragile balance today as is every other wilderness on the planet. There are dangers from open-pit mining, from pulp mills, from logging, and simply from the fearful encroaching sprawl of mankind.

There are over 40 species of plants, birds, and mammals in British Columbia on a list produced by the Committee on the Status of Endangered Wildlife in Canada. Three animal species in British Columbia have the dubious honor of being listed as officially endangered under the provincial Wildlife Act — the Vancouver Island marmot, the burrowing owl, and the sea otter. (The Dawson woodland caribou was once found in the Queen Charlotte Islands. Its status today is final: Extinct.)

British Columbia, with so much beauty to protect, is home to many concerned individuals and environmental groups. The largest organization is probably the British Columbia Federation of Naturalists. The British Columbia Wildlife Federation is very active, sponsoring many projects and land acquisitions. Other groups include Greenpeace, which originated in Vancouver; the powerful Western Canada Wilderness Committee; Valhalla Wilderness Society, in the Kootenays; and the Sierra Club.

An interesting and effective low-key group is the Friends of Ecological Reserves. The reserves are distinctive ecosystems established by orders-in-council for study purposes, or to preserve rare or endangered plants, animals, and land formations. Volunteer wardens work with the government to monitor the reserves, of which there are well over a hundred to date.

Long ago, "when the world was young," as many Indian legends begin, there were supernatural animals, animals on a higher spiritual plane than man. Emissaries of a deeper world, they were thought to act as guides, leading man into the spirit world, and also into a right relationship with this everyday world. There are image-truths in the old legends. Wildlife photographer Joey Walker, who escaped the city years ago for a life in the Okanagan Highlands, puts it simply: "Animals make us feel we belong to this world."

# *The*
# COAST:
## *Ocean, Shore,*
## *and Rain Forest*

*"Nothing can be more beautiful than the effect of the evergreen madronas [arbutus] mixed with the firs, and overhanging calm waters of the gulf lying between the great island and the mainshore — a sea full of lovely islands of all shapes and sizes. Imagine several of the outer Hebrides linked together and covered with fine wood. . .and the Scots mainland magnified into a Switzerland, and you have the British Columbia coast."*

— The Marquis of Lorne, Governor-General of Canada, in *Canadian Pictures*, 1885.

It was a gentle portion of the northwest coast that Lord Lorne was writing about over a century ago, that portion around Victoria, sheltered from Pacific storms by the bulk of the island, characterized by red-brick-colored arbutus trees twisted into fantastic shapes on rocky islets.

*Continued on page 14.*

◀ *Pod of killer whales, off west coast, Vancouver Island*     11

*Killer whale breeching.*

In 1982, a subtidal ecological
reserve was established at
Robson Bight in Johnstone Strait
to protect an important
killer-whale habitat.
Every summer, pods of whales
come to this spot off northeastern
Vancouver Island to rub on the
gravel beaches. There are strict
regulations for whale watchers
entering the sanctuary.

*Killer whales, off west coast, Vancouver Island.*

The entire coast, from the 49th parallel to Portland Inlet at the Alaska border, is about 800 kilometres long; but it's a fjord coast, severely indented with bays, inlets, sounds, and passages, some very extenuated. Burke Channel in to Bella Coola is 85 kilometres long; Knight Inlet is 96 kilometres. If the coastline were straightened out, it would be 27,000 kilometres long. The sides of some of the fjords rise steep and sharp,

*Continued on page 18.*

GRAHAM OSBORNE

THOMAS KITCHIN

*Common murres, west coast, Vancouver Island.*

14

*The Alaskan current brings cold water along the coast,*
*while currents from the south much farther out to sea are warm.*
*These can carry an assortment of surprises*
*— tuna, swordfish, sea turtles, even the great white shark —*
*some of which find their way to inshore areas.*

*Sea lions off the Broken Islands.*

These cold northern waters provide extraordinary visibility, intense color, and an astounding profusion of life. The cold also produces giantism: divers regularly meet jumbo-size anemones, octopus, barnacles, chitons, wolf-eels, and nudibranchs.

*Wolf eel and tiger rockfish, off Campbell River.*

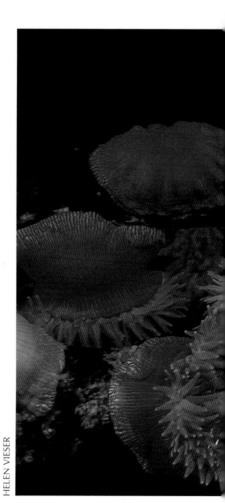

*Octopus in waters off Earls Cove, Sunshine Coast.*

16

*Seastars, Desolation Sound.*

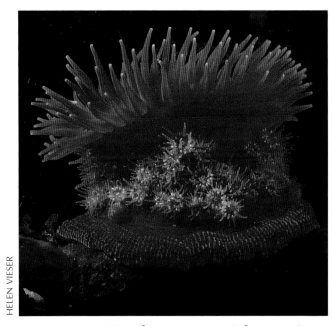

*Brooding anemone, Johnstone Strait.*

*Cluster of anemones, near Port Hardy.*

17

*Black bears on Queen Charlotte Islands.*

so the water is narrowly entrenched in immediate mountain. And the mountains are clothed in the dripping greens of the rain forests that have

been nurtured in the mild, moist Pacific air.

This ragged edge of the continent still teems with life, under the water, on the water, pecking at the shoreline, or hiding in the quiet, heavy, coastal forest. These cold, northern waters are considered one of the premier diving areas of the world. Visibility can be phenomenal, and the colors have a startling clarity. There are five Pacific salmon species. All five of these species are represented among the 10 million salmon that return to the Fraser River each year to spawn. About 300 million young salmon migrate out into the ocean later.

There are 28 marine mammal species: big, blubbery northern sea lions, sea otters, dolphins, and porpoises, harbor and fur seals. About 30 pods of killer whales, with a total population of some 300, live year-round in waters between British Columbia and Washington State. Recent

*Continued on page 29.*

*Grizzly bear, Thompson Sound.* ▶

*Elephant seals off Vancouver Island's west coast.*

GRAHAM OSBORNE

*The shoreline is a transition area between two worlds, where land creatures meet sea creatures, and encounters become uneasy minglings of predator and prey.*

*Black bear.*

*Sea otters off northern Vancouver Island.*

*Tufted puffins, Cleland Island.*

*Brant geese at Clayoquot Sound.*

Wiped out on the British Columbia coast at the turn of the century,
sea otters were reintroduced from Alaska in the late 1960s and early 1970s.
About 650 fuzzy-faced 'clowns of the sea' are back swimming the reefs
and kelp beds along the outer edge of Vancouver Island.

*Oystercatcher with mussel.*

*Rufus hummingbird.*

24

*Great blue heron on giant kelp.*

Unmistakable on the
beach is the oystercatcher,
crow-sized and crow-colored,
sporting long pink legs,
and a red bill
that's relentlessly
dexterous with shellfish.
The great blue heron
can deal a lethal stab
with its powerful beak,
as can the
dainty hummingbird.

*Black-tailed doe at Bedwell River.*

*Barn owl, Boundary Bay.*

*Northern pintail in coastal marsh.*

*White-tailed buck in fireweed.*

*Bald eagles.*

*Eagles occupy
the same nest site
year after year,
adding new layers
of sticks and weeds
each season. In time,
these nests become
huge, weighing
up to one tonne.*

*Bald eagles.*

*Bald eagle protecting nest.*

studies have found, interestingly, that resident orca feed almost entirely on fish, while transients eat other marine mammals as well.

Spring is brought in with the return of the Pacific grey whales from their wintering grounds in the Baja. February through April, some 21,000 of these massive animals swim north to the high Arctic, hugging the shores. Fifteen metres long, weighing 30,000 kilograms, migrating whales cruise at 2 to 8 km-h, although it's realized now that not all are in that much of a hurry. Many linger around on Vancouver Island's west coast all summer, even all year. What the whale watcher gets to see, if lucky, is tails and flippers on a clear, calm day; spume on a stormy day. The sight of a breeching grey whale is remembered for life.

Whale watching is such a part of coastal life that there are whale hot lines so that public sightings — date, time, location, type of whale, number, direction of travel — can be quickly reported.

In some ways, the most interesting part of the coast is the shoreline, the transition area between two worlds, where a mink swims out to catch a crab, or a great white shark washes up from the deep (it's not common, but has happened). It's on the shore where rain forest and ocean meet, where rivers tumble out into the salt. It's where gulls drop clams from the sky to smash them on the rocks below. It's where a grizzly comes out of the forest for a look-see, or perhaps, at a river's mouth, for a bit of fishing.

*Migrating western sandpipers.*

The western sandpiper is one of the three tiniest 'pipers on the coast. It wings through on its annual migration, from breeding grounds in the Arctic, to comfortable wintering spots anywhere from California to Peru. The bittern adds a note of mystery to fresh-water and tidal marshes, wintering over in the Fraser River delta. Its hollow plonk-di-plonk carries a long way.

30

*American bittern.*

31

*California bighorn sheep above Vaseux Lake.*

# *The* DRYLANDS:

## *Bunch-grass, Desert, and Sagebrush*

*"It is a land that drew me like a magnet into its soul."*

— Richard Hobson, pioneer rancher, Chilcotins.

The drylands are all the hot, interior parts of the province that suggest "Home on the Range," ranchlands, roundups, and saddles. The drylands are where the sage is pungent, the hills roll, and there are puffs of dust under a horse's hoof. It's where a friend's dog got bit by a rattler, on Anarchist Mountain, trying to protect the horses. It was a blue heeler, good kind of dog for this kind of country; just didn't know about rattlesnakes. Everyone says rattlesnakes don't bother you. Bit the dog though. (Yes, it died.)

It's hard country, but full of romance.

Ranching and farming began during the 1860s, and several large ranches grew in the

*Bighorn lambs at play, Vaseux Lake.*

rich bunch-grass country along the middle Fraser and lower Chilcotin. The nucleus of the famous Gang Ranch was established by Jerome and Thadeus Harper in the early 1860s; the Alkali Lake ranch was founded in 1861.

The rangelands cover a vast area of central British Columbia, through the Cariboo-Chilcotin region, south through the Okanagan to the American border. The hottest part of this dry belt is in the valley bottoms, where vegetation is limited to bunch-grass and drought-resistant shrubs like rabbit-brush, antelope-brush (in the South Okanagan), and sage.

A landmark tree is the yellow or ponderosa pine, which is able to withstand high temperatures in the seedling stage. It prefers open space, and will follow the grassland up to the plateaus as long as there isn't too much rainfall. At higher elevations generally, the air is cooler, it retains moisture, and there is growth — aspens, Douglas fir, lodgepole pine. These

"parklands," or "uplands," along with the dry belts in the valley floors, make up rangelands.

In the summer, deer prefer the higher areas of rangelands (they come down into the valleys in winter). White-tailed deer in particular like a fringe habitat, an open space for browsing near enough to a thicket for safety. White-tails especially like areas that have been strip-logged, because they have a secret penchant for black tree moss, and will even leave an alfalfa field to get it. Mule deer like wide open spaces more than the white-tails. And everywhere the deer do go, the cougar is sure to follow.

In the last century, the lowland hills were covered with bunch-grass — tall, rich clumps of perennial grasses. However, bunch-grass didn't stand up to grazing (even a hundred years ago it didn't). Coarser varieties of grasses, like needle-and-thread and cheat grass, took its place, and in some places, undesirable species

*Continued on page 38.*

*California bighorn sheep, Vaseux Lake.* ▶

G. PATRICK GREEN

*This dry land is open, and if you're quiet and watch closely, you will see much, not the timid rattlesnake probably, but the non-venomous garter snake for sure. The warm, shallow, alkaline lakes offer sanctuary to water birds.*

*Golden-mantled ground squirrel, Selkirk Mountains.*

VICTORIA HURST

*Rattlesnake in south Okanagan Valley.*

36

*Mallard ducks.*

*Garter snake near Terrace.*

37

THOMAS KITCHIN

*White-tailed buck.*

like knapweed have truly taken over, presenting serious problems. Sagebrush itself may not be popular with the rancher, but is romantic and aromatic for the visitor, and provides scrub shelter for important wildlife.

Inhospitable as this dryland may sound, dozens of creatures are perfectly adapted and do like it hot: coyotes, gophers, badgers, mule deer, and foxes; songbirds, game birds, and raptors; lizards and toads. The endangered burrowing owl is being carefully nurtured by a recovery team.

*Continued on page 44.*

*Deer are happiest
in fringe habitat,
where they can munch
the tasty grasses,
yet melt into
the forest at first
scent of danger.*

THOMAS KITCHIN

*White-tailed deer, Creston Valley.*

*White-tailed deer, Creston Valley.* ▶

*Burrowing owl, Bummers Flats.*

*Badger in grasslands, southeast British Columbia.*

*Mule deer, Cathedral Provincial Park.*

41

*Cougar, southern British Columbia.*

42

*Roughed grouse drumming.*

*Turkey vulture near Vaseux Lake.*

Agriculture had systematically worked on eliminating the gopher holes and badger burrows where the pigeon-sized owl lived, until all breeding birds were extirpated. The reintroduction of breeding birds with young is proving successful. The burrowing owl is slowly increasing.

The thriving orchards of Osoyoos and Oliver near the border are heavily irrigated, but where the sprinklers stop, sagebrush, antelopebrush, and prickly pear cactus begin in what is the most desertlike part of this arid zone. Actually the northern fringe of the American Great Basin Desert, this pocket desert is the hottest place in the country, reaching a blistering 44 degrees Celsius.

Many of the plants and animals here are rare or unique in Canada: the Great Basin spadefoot toad, canyon wren, sage thrasher, Brewer's sparrow, northern Pacific rattlesnake. Creepy crawlies include unique species of tiger beetles, scarabs, and butterflies; also praying mantises, black-widow spiders, and scorpions. Overhead cruise the skin-headed turkey vultures, a sinister V-shape in the sky, vetting the ground below for carrion. They never kill; only eat what's dead. They are the final monitors, keeping the land picked clean and dry.

*"There is a small sized wolf [coyote], called the medicine wolf, regarded by the Indians as a sort of manitou."*
— Father Pierre-Jean de Smet, from a letter Sept. 10, 1841.

*Young coyote, southeast British Columbia.*

*Coyote in wildflowers, East Kootenay.*

Canada geese over eastern Chilcotin marshland.

## The
# WETLANDS:

### Valleys, Marshes, and Sloughs

*"After a sojourn among the more elevated snowfields, the return to the fertility and plenty of the lower valleys is refreshing in the highest degree. The sudden change from eternal winter to the beauty of spring, from spring to summer, from the abodes of overwhelming chaos to fairer scenes, from death as it were into life. . .the wearied traveller yields himself up to the. . .touch of love and beauty."*

— Edmund Coleman, Artist.

*Harper's New Monthly Magazine,* November 1869.

Edmund Coleman was a painter and mountaineer who came to British Columbia for a visit in the 1860s and stayed for 10 years. He loved the mountains, or so he said, but his word-painting favors the life-giving valleys.

*Continued on page 51.*

*Black-tailed buck, Canal Flats.*

The range of the
marsh hawk is
holarctic. From here
to Siberia and
Sweden, it can be
seen gliding low
over fields, meadows,
and marshes,
on the hunt
for small rodents.

*Dive-bombing marsh hawk, South Okanagan.*

*Elk calf, Columbia Valley.*

49

*House finch on crabapple, Fraser River estuary.*

◄ *Steller's jay in skunk cabbage patch.*

There is no particular area in British Columbia called "the Wetlands." Wetlands are everywhere — every lush, green valley from Cowichan to Creston, every swamp and slough from the Fraser River delta to Bummers Flats near historic Fort Steele, and the moose-viewing

*Barrow's goldeneye.*

areas north of Prince George. Where there are lakes and rivers, there are wetlands, and the wetlands are flush with life.

The most striking valley in the province, in fact in North America, is the Rocky Mountain Trench, which runs generally north-south (strictly speaking, northwest-southeast), defined by the Rockies on the east, the Columbia Mountains on the west. The trench, or "the Valley," as locals call it, is geologically unique. Visible from space, it is a significant feature of the planet, over 1,600 kilometres long, varying from 3 to 16 kilometres wide. The valley has been hospitable for thousands of years: the Kootenay Indians were living and hunting here as early as 10,000 BC.

There are no other interior wetlands in the province of comparable size or supporting such diversity of wildlife as the Columbia River wetlands, the East Kootenay section of the Rocky Mountain Trench. BC Environment is currently proposing a Wildlife Management Area be established for the entire Columbia wetlands.

In the 20,235 hectares of marsh between Canal Flats and Golden, some 272 species of birds have been recorded. This is a major breeding area for bald eagles, ospreys, and great blue herons. About 30 kilometres north of Radium is a heron

Continued on page 56.

PAUL LALLY

*American coot, Columbia River wetlands.*

*Green-backed heron near White Rock.* ▶

*Osprey nest site, Creston Lake.*

*Yellow-headed blackbird in Okanagan wetlands.*

*Wood duck, Kootenay Lake.*

*Male cinnamon teal near Cranbrook.*

*Moose foraging on Bowron River marsh.*

rookery. The 300 pairs of herons nesting here make it the second largest concentration in western Canada. In other areas, nest boxes have been set up for wood duck, common goldeneye, and others. In some places Canada geese nest on top of muskrat houses (the muskrat don't eat the eggs). Here we find a potpourri of ornithological delights: red-tailed hawk, white-throated swift, mountain bluebird, northern flicker, hairy woodpecker, ruddy duck, black tern, Wilson's phalarope; sandhill cranes migrating through.

Among mammals, the valley supports large populations of elk and deer, and is an important wintering area for Rocky Mountain bighorn sheep. Residents include moose, mountain goat, black bear, grizzly, cougar, bobcat, and coyote. Muskrat and beaver are abundant: their lodges can be seen in backwater marshes. The badger is seen occasionally.

Amphibians include the widely distributed western toad, spotted frog, and wood frog; and also the local northern leopard frog, and northern long-toed salamander. There are garter snakes, painted turtles, and the secretive rubber boa.

In the flats south of Kootenay Lake, where the Kootenay River overflows its banks each spring, is the Creston Valley Wildlife Management Area, a 6,880-hectare bird and

*Continued on page 61.*

56

*Cow moose and calf, Dease Lake marsh.*

*Moose, Dease Lake area.*

*Butterfly on fireweed.*

*Eared grebe on floating nest, Spillimacheen River marsh.*

58

*Nesting red-necked grebe, Bowron River marsh.*

*Marshland is a great provider, and every wetland from the Fraser delta to the Creston flats is alive with busy creatures — building nests, cutting trees, or just fishing.*

G. PATRICK GREEN

*Red-winged blackbirds in Columbia River wetlands.*

*Beaver carrying willow branch across Rocky Mountain lake.*

60

waterfowl refuge protecting some 250 species of paddlers, waders, raptors, and songbirds. About 9,000 hectares of this floodplain have been dyked to create fertile farmland: the entire area is an awe-inspiring sight.

Farther north, in the areas of Kamloops Lake, Shuswap, and the other large lakes, there are hundreds of smaller lakes and marshes that provide valuable stopovers as well as nesting sites for thousands of waterfowl. Besides an incredible variety of puddle ducks, divers and dabblers, several large species grace these skies — trumpeter and whistling swans, Canada geese, snow geese, and pelicans.

There is a success story at remote Stum Lake in the Chilcotins. More than one hundred

*Black-crowned night heron, Okanagan Lake.*

*Black tern drops stickleback to youngster, McQueen Slough, northeast British Columbia.*

*Turtles in Creston Valley marsh.*

62

pairs of white pelicans — British Columbia's only colony — have been safely breeding within the protected confines of White Pelican Provincial Park, which has no road access.

Designated as threatened from 1976 - 1986, the white pelican was officially delisted four years ago by the Committee on the Status of Endangered Wildlife in Canada (COSEWIC).

*Immature red-tailed hawk.*

*Sockeye salmon struggle up Babine River rapids.*

64

*Adams River stained red with sockeye salmon run.*

Spectators travel from
around the world to witness
the phenomenon of spawning
salmon in British Columbia.
The salmon returns from
the open sea to lay its eggs
in the exact stream
where its own life began.
The fish are driven by
the specific water chemistry
of their home streams.
Each stream has its own
'finger print'.

# The
# MOUNTAINS:

## Forest, Meadow, and Alpine Crag

*"The snow-topped mountains, seen from the plains like the tents of giants pitched to contend man's westward way, would be pierced again. . . . Surveys were sent out to find the way, to besiege the fortress of the mountains, to follow rivers and to pause by lakes, set like moats below rocky walls."*
— Howard O'Hagan, *Tay John*, 1960.

"That inhospitable country, that sea of mountains," complained Edward Blake, premier of Ontario, in 1874. But it was not entirely inhospitable to the mountain men of O'Hagan's classic novel, nor to the dozens of animals and birds that find a haven in the heights.

Three-quarters of British Columbia lies 1,000 metres and more above sea level, in a succession of mountain ranges. The two maritime

◄ *Bighorn sheep, Rocky Mountains.*

67

ranges are more rugged, and even more spectacular, many think, than the Rockies. The Coast Mountains on the mainland are the highest in North America. Stepping out yet farther west, the outer mountain range begins with the St. Elias Mountains on the Alaska border, south through the Queen Charlotte Islands to form the backbone of Vancouver Island. Fairweather Mountain, one of the St. Elias peaks, is the highest point in British Columbia, at 4,663 metres.

Lining up north-south in formidable succession to the Rockies are the three parallel ranges of the Columbia Mountains: the Purcells, the Selkirks, and the Monashees (east to west). The Cariboo Range to the north makes up the Columbia package. Between the Columbia Mountains and the Rockies, and the mountains of the coast, is the rolling interior plateau, which has its own complement of mountains and valleys, uplands and lowlands. It is a complex landscape.

In the province's southern half, the tree line occurs at about 2,000 metres: beyond this point, trees give up. In northern British Columbia, with the much lower temperatures, the tree line

*Richardson ground squirrels, Rocky Mountains.*

*Young Rocky Mountain bighorn ram at salt lick.*

*When two evenly matched rams decide to battle it out, the head-bashing can be an awesome and long-drawn-out process. With a thickened bone at the point of impact, rams can survive over three dozen blasting encounters in a day.*

*Bighorn rams on Rocky Mountain meadow.*

69

occurs at 900 metres. Because there is a substantial difference of degree, of intensity, between the northern areas and the southern (albeit they are both alpine), the north is treated separately.

A representative mountainous area is Kootenay National Park, which stretches from Vermilion Pass at the continental divide in the Rockies, west 94 kilometres to its southern gate at Radium Hot Springs. East of the continental divide (which also divides British Columbia and

MYRON KOZAK

Alberta), all water flows to Hudson Bay; to the west all water flows to the Pacific. In 1985, Kootenay National Park, along with the other Rockies' parks — Banff, Jasper, and Yoho — was declared a World Heritage Site.

Kootenay has more than spectacular landscape: it is the only national park containing both cactus and glaciers. Wildlife viewing, therefore, is also varied and significant. Elk, mule and white-tailed deer, bighorn sheep, mountain goats, moose, and black bears can often be seen from the highway. Back apace are coyotes, wolves,

*Continued on page 75.*

*Mountain goat tracks through snows of Brian Boru Peak, near Smithers.*

Mountain goats inhabit the roughest possible terrain,
usually at or around the timberline, where they
manage even in winter to find a few frozen shrubs
and a little dried grass to nibble on.

*Mountain goats in Stikine Canyon.* ▶

PAUL LALLY

*Mountain goat nanny and kid, Vermilion Range.*

*Grey jays in Englemann spruce tree, Rocky Mountains.*

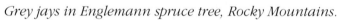

THOMAS KITCHIN

72

THOMAS KITCHIN

*Hoary marmots, Manning Park.*

*Vancouver Island marmots in Nanaimo Lakes watershed.*

G. PATRICK GREEN

74

and grizzly bears. Columbian and golden-mantled ground squirrels and chipmunks, along with grey jays and Clarke's nutcrackers, are happy campers. Alpine meadows can offer such treats as vivid blue larkspur, red paintbrush, buttercups, white bunchberry.

Bighorn and thinhorn sheep flourish in British Columbia, and both are related to the mouflons of the Mediterranean and other wild sheep of the world through Asia Minor and South Central Asia. Generally, bighorns are found south of the 55th parallel; thinhorns north of the 55th (see next chapter).

The Rocky Mountain bighorn is the classic, found in the Rockies and in scattered bands north of Mount Robson. The California bighorn, a similar subspecies, roams the Okanagan, Similkameen, and South Chilcotin regions. Mountain sheep prefer grasslands, in the rain shadows of mountains, and in winter require areas of light snow where they can paw for food easily. Thus they are found on lower elevations, and on windswept, south-facing slopes, especially slopes within easy reach of rugged cliffs, their escape hatches from predators.

It is sometimes said, "Sheep on one mountain, goats on another," to suggest an innate animosity between the two. Not necessarily so. They like a different terrain, and the bighorn's habitat is positively comfy compared

*Lynx.*

*Cougar, Rocky Mountains.*

with the mountain goat's. Related to a small group of mountain antelopes (it's actually neither a sheep nor a goat), the mountain goat chooses the roughest possible terrain, usually remaining at or above the timberline, on steep ledges or dizzying crags. They can fall prey to cougars, coyotes, wolves, bobcats, even wolverines, but are equipped for escape with cushioned skid-proof pads on their little black hooves. If push comes to shove, their stiletto-like hollow horns can be wicked.

The unpredictable bear is everywhere. Grizzlies shun human company, but the smaller black bear — which can vary from jet black through cinnamon and blond — is all too

*Cougar, Akamina—Kishinena Recreation Area, southeast corner of British Columbia.*

GORDON PEACHEY

*Solitary bobcat, Okanagan Highlands.*

*The bobcat is a solitary, silent predator, hunter of small game. Weighing an average 13 kilograms, the bobcat is slightly smaller than its northern cousin, the lynx, and it is also more adaptable to changing habitat, an inveterate survivor.*

gregarious. It is also an agile tree climber. A large black bear can be bigger than a small grizzly, but there are other distinguishing marks. The black has a straight back line, while the grizzly has a prominent shoulder hump formed by the muscles of the massive front legs. The black has rather flat feet with short curved claws; the grizzly has long curved claws.

Grizzlies and black bears occur throughout forested and mountainous regions. There is

*Prowling bobcat, Okanagan Highlands.*

*Marten, Coast Mountains.*

*Great grey owl, northern Rocky Mountains.*

one bear, however, that has a specific locale, and is unmistakable: the legendary white Kermode (pronounced ker-mo-dee), or "snow bear." Called "Kodie Kermode" by locals, the bear inhabits a small range of 400 square kilometres in the area of Terrace, Hazelton, and Kitimat. Discovered about 1900, the Kermode was eventually established as a subspecies of black bear, coming in many hues from chestnut red, orange, yellow, and gold, to bluish-grey, brown, and black, or a

*Bull elk in mist.*

*Kermode bear in Skeena River forest.*

mix of black, brown and white. It's the white one that created the mystery. A hunting ban on white Kermodes was reinstated in 1965.

Concluding on a small (furry) note: the endangered, chocolate-colored Vancouver Island marmot, a woodchuck lookalike, living only on Vancouver Island, has been assigned a recovery team. The marmot inhabits logged and alpine areas on the southern half of the island, and the team is working to increase what is the world's entire population. At the moment, there are only about 300 of these little animals.

*In the north, everything that grows, every creature that grazes or browses, rips or tears must cope with short summers and long, intensely cold winters. The eco-link is the pale sun, the silver cold.*

*Moose 'yarded up' in mid-winter, Stewart-Cassiar region.*

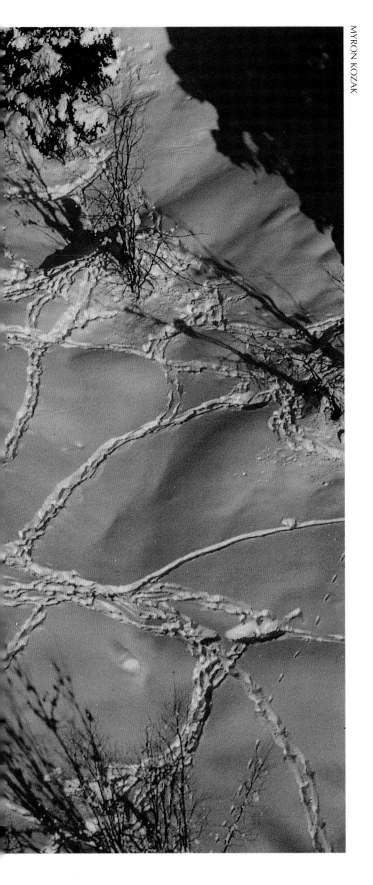

## *The*
# NORTH:
### *Wheatlands, Mountains, and Muskeg*

*"The archetypal Canadian landscape is one laden with conifer forests spreading out across an endless, white expanse of frozen lakes and rivers. The sturdy spruce, pine and fir endure icy blizzards and give shelter to wildlife. The air crackles with the cold, and both the nights and the winter seem to go on forever."*

— Cameron Young, *The Forests of British Columbia*, 1985.

This boreal or northern forest extends from the eastern shores of Newfoundland right across Canada, sweeping into northern British Columbia. Boreas was the Greek god of the north wind, so a boreal forest is not merely "northern," it is a forest "shaped by the north wind." And so it is — a seemingly endless wilderness of forest and muskeg and, in some places, permafrost.

85

*Rocky Mountain bighorn ewe and lamb, Spatsizi Plateau.*

The physical setting within British Columbia, however, varies more widely than one would suspect. In the west lie the great mountains of the Coast range, then the Skeena and Cassiar mountains, and the plateaus between, similar to the rest of the province.

But the eastern section is a surprise, splitting into three distinct zones — the northern Rocky Mountain Trench (the broad valley extending 1,600 kilometres north from Montana), the Rockies themselves, and then — lo and behold! — level plains. This is all because the northern reaches of the Rocky Mountains cut west on a dramatic diagonal. They do not form the entire boundary between British Columbia and Alberta.

The Interior Plain thus created in the northeast is almost as large as England, and with its grain elevators, and its chinooks and blizzards, it has more in common with Canada's Prairies than it does with British Columbia. In fact the Peace River area was not even accessible from the rest of the province until 1952, when the John

*Stone sheep, Muncho Lake Provincial Park.*

The stone sheep of the north are thinhorns, related to wild sheep
throughout many mountainous areas of the world from the
Mediterranean and Asia Minor through south-central Asia and Siberia.
In British Columbia, they only occur north of the 55th parallel.

*Mule deer buck.*

Hart Highway connected Prince George and Dawson Creek. Until then, all commerce moved east-west across the top of the world, and in the very early days, the Peace (via Edmonton) was a gateway to the Klondike gold fields.

This northern plain was a natural gold mine for wildlife, too. Alexander Mackenzie wintered over in 1792 - 93, on his way to becoming the first European explorer to cross North America. He wrote, "This magnificent theatre of nature has all the decorations which the trees and animals of the country can afford it: groves of poplars in every shape vary the scene; and their intervals are enlivened with vast herds of elks and buffaloes. . .The country is so crowded with animals as to have the appearance, in some places, of a stall-yard."

The naturalist today will find moose, white-tailed and mule deer, woodland caribou and grizzly bear, black bear, wolves and coyotes, fishers, martens, mink, porcupine, river otters, lynx, snowshoe hares, beaver, and muskrat, for starters. Nesting species of birds include bald eagles, ospreys, goshawks, great grey owls,

*Mule deer.* ▶

three-toed woodpeckers, yellow rails, and many warblers. In this corner of British Columbia only flies the eastern blue jay (elsewhere is the indigo-blue Steller's jay, official provincial bird, and the cheeky "whiskey jack" of the mountains). Migrations bring rafts of loons, sandhill cranes, tundra swans, geese, ducks, and shorebirds.

Meanwhile, away from the wheatlands and back in the boreal forest live some of the province's largest, and most interesting, animals.

The moose is the largest member of the deer family. Potentially very dangerous, a mature bull can stand higher at the shoulder than any saddle horse, and weigh in at over 800 kilograms. It will tree a man, and hang around below with the patience of Job. Up to 1900, moose lived mostly in the north, but as forests were cut, and huge areas opened up for settling, more moose were attracted south. Thriving on the tasty forage

*Continued on page 95.*

PAUL LALLY

*Great horned owl.*

90

*Bison with calf, northeastern British Columbia.* ▶

*Grizzly bear, northern Rockies.*

*Grizzly sow and cub.*

in burn areas and cleared patches, greater numbers of them reached Barkerville by 1901, Williams Lake by 1923, Vernon and Princeton in the '30s.

While moose distribution has ironically increased because of man's activities, the range of the woodland caribou has unfortunately been reduced, especially in southeastern British Columbia. A beautiful animal (the caribou and the reindeer of northern Europe and Siberia belong to a single circumpolar species), it requires a continuous range, and is highly vulnerable to local disturbance and destruction of habitat. Unlike the barren-ground caribou of the far north, our woodland species do not form

*Grizzly in northern stream.* ▶

THOMAS KITCHIN

*Wolf in northern grassland.*

they have the mountain sheep's characteristic golden eye. Stone sheep are slightly heavier, and very dark except for white on the face, belly, inside legs, and rump patch.

There are bison in British Columbia's north, but only the plains variety. Historically, the larger, darker, woollier wood bison probably occurred throughout the northeast and into the Yukon, but now this subspecies tends to be northeast of British Columbia in the Athabasca Valley, and Alberta's Wood Buffalo National Park. Meanwhile, a well-known herd of plains bison (known as *Bison bison bison*) can be seen in the Rocky Mountain foothills at Pink Mountain, near old Mile 143 on the Alaska Highway. They had escaped captivity, and are now living wild and extremely well, thank you very much.

large herds, but move about in small groups, liking the seclusion of the forest. In winter they will feed on lichens or "beard mosses" pulled from the lower branches of the conifers.

Living north of the 55th parallel are the two subspecies of thinhorn sheep, the Dall's and the stone sheep. With both, the horns are lighter than the massive bighorn's, but have a much wider spreading spiral. Dall's are the only white wild sheep in the world, but they're not albino:

Where there is prey, there are predators: lynx, grizzlies, coyotes, and wolves. Grizzlies occur in many parts of the province, but in the north, it is commonly thought that there are more of them. The area from Pine Pass Summit to Chetwynd, for example, is said to have the highest grizzly-to-people ratio in British Columbia. This may of course be a comment on how few people live in this particular stretch.

*Mountain caribou, Mount Robson Provincial Park.*

Grey wolves are seldom seen by man, though they are said to be "moderate to plentiful" in coastal areas like western Vancouver Island, and in the north. They are absent from the Queen Charlotte Islands. They have certainly been exterminated from large blocks of the south province, but range north right up to the Arctic Archipelago. The wolf has always been fascinating to mankind, especially because of its complex social structure, and the considerable responsibility each pack member assumes.

A wolf can bring almost anything down. Mule deer have been seen as far north as the Liard River Valley, but they don't last long. A mulie is nice prey for a wolf, just about its own size. Its normal prey is moose. A deer is nice and easy, and as most things are hard in the north, a deer is very welcome.

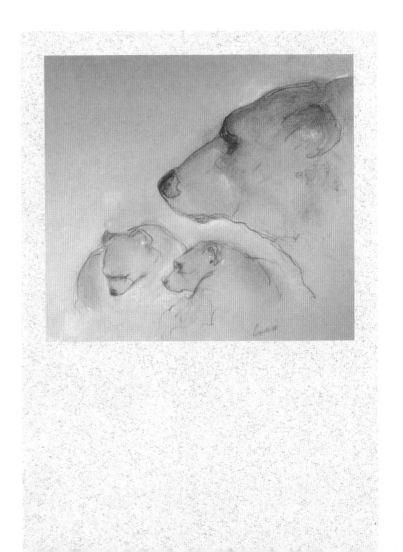

*Red fox in Kispiox Valley.*

*Snowy owl.*

96

*Woodland caribou, northeastern British Columbia.*